منهَجُ الحَقِّ

Manhaj al-Ḥaqq
The Way of Truth

Shaykh ʿAbd al-Raḥmān b. Nāṣir al-Saʿdi

Poetic Rendering
John N. Starling III

2nd Edition, al-Muḥarram 1439 | October 2017

ISBN: 978-0692961278

Table of Contents

بسم الله الرحمن الرحيم

In the name of God.

Preface

I begin by praising Allāh and sending prayers of peace and blessing upon the last and final Prophet and Messenger, Muḥammad.

In your hands is the scholarly poem of the erudite scholar, jurist, and exegete Shaykh ʿAbd al-Raḥmān b. Nāṣir al- Saʿdi, entitled Manhaj al-Ḥaqq, translated as The Way of Truth. This poem consists of issues pertaining to the Islamic creed and manners of its spirituality.

It should be clearly understood that my translation of this work is not a word-for-word translation, but a "poetic" rendering. Poetic license was taken on the rare occasion when needed. Therefore, I do acknowledge that certain minor sacrifices were made to maintain the rhyming nature of the poem in English, but believe they were necessary to deliver this work as done so by its author. I have made great efforts to preserve the intent of the author, while maintaining a rhythmic structure, and in doing so have relied heavily upon scholarly explanations of this work.

In conclusion, I ask Allāh to bless you, the reader, and guide you to that which He loves and is pleased with. I also ask Allāh to bless the author of this work and all those who have serviced it, and that He forgive me of my faults and make this a good deed on my scale the day I return to Him.

About the Author

The great scholar Shaykh 'Abd al-Raḥmān b. Nāṣir b. 'Abd Allāh b. Nāṣir b. Ḥamad al-Tamīmi al-Najdi al-Ḥanabli al-Sa'di was born on the 12ᵗʰ of Muḥarram, 1307H in the city of 'Unayzah, al-Qaṣīm. He grew up as an orphan in extremely difficult social and economic times.

As a young boy, he displayed both the tenacity and passion required to seek Islamic knowledge. Before the age of 12 he completed memorizing the Qur'ān in its entirety. He benefited from the local scholars as well as those in the surrounding regions to such a degree that he was recognized as having achieved the unexpected for a young man of his age. He solely dedicated his time to studying the Islamic sciences with interests in Ḥadīth, Uṣūl, Fiqh, Tafsīr, 'Aqīdah, and Arabic. Though he had numerous teachers, he was greatly influenced by the works of Shaykh al-Islām Ibn Taymiyyah and his student Ibn al-Qayyim.

He was a true leader of his age and known to champion the issues of his people both socially and academically. He was a prolific teacher and author whose legacy continues to live to this very day.

Introduction

The science of creed is referred to by some of the greats as al-Fiqh al-Akbar. It is the foundation upon which the faithful worship The Divine. Without adopting the true creed, the seeker will find themselves wandering astray, lost to their own limited devices.

While an in-depth study of creed is of paramount importance, it truly comes to life through spiritual endeavor. Only when coupled with a guided practice of worship, driven by love of The Merciful, will the believer's soul be satisfied and heart be filled with His remembrance.

In this precise poem, the author has managed to embody the most essential elements of both creed and spiritual manner in a way that mesmerizes the ear and captivates the heart. Upon a thorough study of this text, the true seeker will be well-equipped to embark upon their journey to Allāh and the home of the Hereafter.

The Way of Truth

Seek, sincere searcher of the truthful way,

the nation's manner to achieve delight.

Ponder, God guide you, on what I portray.

Reflect like he who intended what's right.

We confess, our Lord, no other there is

He's praised and exalted above the throne.

We witness that our devotion is His

our submissive love is for Him alone.

فَيَا سَائِلًا عَنْ مَنْهَجِ الْحَقِّ يَبْتَغِي

سُلُوكَ طَرِيقِ الْقَوْمِ حَقًّا وَيَسْعَدُ

تَأَمَّلْ هَدَاكَ اللهُ مَا قَدْ نَظَمْتُهُ

تَأَمَّلَ مَنْ قَدْ كَانَ لِلْحَقِّ يَقْصِدُ

نُقِرُّ بِأَنَّ اللهَ لَا رَبَّ غَيْرُهُ

إِلَهٌ عَلَى الْعَرْشِ الْعَظِيمِ مُمَجَّدُ

وَنَشْهَدُ أَنَّ اللهَ مَعْبُودُنَا الَّذِي

نُخَصِّصُهُ بِالْحُبِّ ذُلًّا وَنُفْرِدُ

For Him is all honor, glory, and praise

and thus everyone, for Him they are bound.

Heaven and earth glorify Him in phrase.

The creatures, they all commend Him profound.

The One exalted, above equal match.

From negative feature, lofty and high.

Attributes we confirm, from His dispatch,

and free from those who construe and deny.

فَلِلَّهِ كُلُّ الْحَمْدِ وَالْمَجْدِ وَالثَّنَا

فَمِنْ أَجْلِ ذَا كُلٌّ إِلَى اللهِ يَقْصِدُ

تُسَبِّحُهُ الْأَمْلَاكُ وَالْأَرْضُ وَالسَّمَا

وَكُلُّ جَمِيعِ الْخَلْقِ حَقًّا وَتَحْمَدُ

تَنَزَّهَ عَنْ نِدٍّ وَكُفْءٍ مُمَاثِلٍ

وَعَنْ وَصْفِ ذِي النُّقْصَانِ جَلَّ الْمُوَحَّدُ

وَنُثْبِتُ أَخْبَارَ الصِّفَاتِ جَمِيعَهَا

وَنَبْرَأُ مِنْ تَأْوِيلِ مَنْ كَانَ يَجْحَدُ

His attributes' essence, the mind can't hold,

so to what the messenger said concede.

The Lofty Eternal, His features extolled.

His lasting refuge, all creatures do need.

Lofty in being, power, and degree.

Close to His servants, answering with love.

Living Sustainer, with bounty, need free.

To Him belongs praise, every kind thereof.

فَلَيْسَ يُطِيقُ الْعَقْلُ كُنْهَ صِفَاتِهِ

فَسَلِّمْ لِمَا قَالَ الرَّسُولُ مُحَمَّدُ

هُوَ الصَّمَدُ الْعَالِي لِعِظَمِ صِفَاتِهِ

وَكُلُّ جَمِيعِ الْخَلْقِ لِلَّهِ يَصْمُدُ

عَلِيٌّ عَلَا ذَاتًا وَقَدْرًا وَقَهْرُهُ

قَرِيبٌ مُجِيبٌ بِالْوَرَى مُتَوَدِّدُ

هُوَ الْحَيُّ وَالْقَيُّومُ ذُو الْجُودِ وَالْغِنَى

وَكُلُّ صِفَاتِ الْحَمْدِ لِلَّهِ تُسْنَدُ

Encompasses all in knowledge and might,

in virtue and grace, it's Him we adore.

The smallest of things He has in His sight,

Observes the servants and hears them for sure.

Over His dominion with praise and reign.

The creatures attest, His wisdom is great.

His descending at night, we do maintain,

the one sent with truth, as Aḥmad did state.

أَحَاطَ بِكُلِّ الْخَلْقِ عِلْمًا وَقُدْرَةً

وَبِرًّا وَإِحْسَانًا فَإِيَّاهُ نَعْبُدُ

وَيُبْصِرُ ذَرَّاتِ الْعَوَالِمِ كُلَّهَا

وَيَسْمَعُ أَصْوَاتَ الْعِبَادِ وَيَشْهَدُ

لَهُ الْمُلْكُ وَالْحَمْدُ الْمُحِيطُ بِمُلْكِهِ

وَحِكْمَتُهُ الْعُظْمَى بِهَا الْخَلْقُ تَشْهَدُ

وَنَشْهَدُ أَنَّ اللَّهَ يَنْزِلُ فِي الدُّجَى

كَمَا قَالَهُ الْمَبْعُوثُ بِالْحَقِّ أَحْمَدُ

We witness, apostles, by Him dispatched,

with signs for creatures, they direct and guide.

Some over others, He made them unmatched.

In wisdom, Alone, Great, and Glorified.

Best of His creatures in heaven or Earth,

Prophet Muḥammad, to guide all creation.

He assigned for him companions of worth,

established true faith, laying foundation.

وَنَشْهَدُ أَنَّ اللهَ أَرْسَلَ رُسُلَهُ

بِآيَاتِهِ لِلْخَلْقِ تَهْدِي وَتُرْشِدُ

وَفَاضَلَ بَيْنَ الرُّسْلِ وَالْخَلْقِ كُلِّهِمْ

بِحِكْمَتِهِ جَلَّ العظِيمُ الْمُوَحَّدُ

فَأَفْضَلُ خَلْقِ اللهِ فِي الْأَرْضِ وَالسَّمَا

نَبِيُّ الهُدَى وَالعَالَمِينَ مُحَمَّدُ

وَخَصَّ لَهُ الرَّحمنُ أَصْحَابَهُ الْأُلَى

أَقَامُوا الهُدَى وَالدِّينَ حَقًّا وَمَهَّدُوا

Loving them all, his companions and kin,

a certain mandate for the faithful folk.

Who say that His speech is most perfect in

the meaning as well as the words He spoke.

His speech, unparalleled, not created,

unlike creature's words, Glorified is He

All good and evil, witnessed and stated,

though man toils and strives, it's by His decree.

نُحِبُّ جَمِيعَ الآلِ وَالصَّحْبِ عِنْدَنَا

مَعَاشِرَ أَهْلِ الْحَقِّ فَرْضٌ مُؤَكَّدُ

وَمِنْ قَوْلِ أَهْلِ الْحَقِّ أَنَّ كَلَامَهُ

هُوَ اللَّفْظُ وَالمَعْنَى جَمِيعًا مُجَوَّدُ

وَلَيْسَ بِمَخْلُوقٍ وَأَنَّى لِخَلْقِهِ

بِقَوْلٍ كَقَوْلِ اللهِ إِذْ هُوَ أَمْجَدُ

وَنَشْهَدُ أَنَّ الْخَيْرَ وَالشَّرَّ كُلَّهُ

بِتَقْدِيرِهِ وَالْعَبْدُ يَسْعَى وَيَجْهَدُ

Our faith is speech, action, and intention.

To righteous good deeds it is confined.

Increased with good and from evil abstention.

With sin it is spoiled and declined.

In the Resurrection, we do believe,

and The Hereafter and all that is found.

Ponder His kingdom in hopes to achieve

guidance from thought in His signs all around.

وَإِيمَانُنَا قَوْلٌ وَفِعْلٌ وَنِيَّةٌ

مِنَ الْخَيْرِ وَالطَّاعَاتِ فِيهَا نُقَيِّدُ

وَيَزْدَادُ بِالطَّاعَاتِ مَعْ تَرْكِ مَا نَهَى

وَيَنْقُصُ بِالعِصْيَانِ جَزْمًا وَيَفْسُدُ

نُقِرُّ بِأَحْوَالِ القِيَامَةِ كُلِّهَا

وَمَا اشْتَمَلَتْهُ الدَّارُ حَقًّا وَنَشْهَدُ

تَفَكَّرْ بِآثَارِ العَظِيمِ وَمَا حَوَتْ

مَمَالِكُهُ العُظْمَى لَعَلَّكَ تَرْشُدُ

17

Have you not seen the night coming so dark

expelled at dawn by an army of rays.

Ponder the sky and its vastness so stark

And its moving stars, so brilliant ablaze.

Does it not have a ruling creator,

unique and alone, all wise and aware?

Certainly so, by the One who made her

As mysteries placed, His witness they bear.

أَلَمْ تَرَ هَذَا اللَّيْلَ إِذْ جَاءَ مُظْلِمًا

فَأَعْقَبَهُ جَيْشٌ مِنَ الصُّبْحِ يَطْرُدُ

تَأَمَّلْ بِأَرْجَاءِ السَّمَاءِ جَمِيعِهَا

كَوَاكِبَهَا وَقَّادَةً تَتَرَدَّدُ

أَلَيْسَ لِهَذَا مُحْدِثٌ مُتَصَرِّفٌ

حَكِيمٌ عَلِيمٌ وَاحِدٌ مُتَفَرِّدُ

بَلَى وَالَّذِي بِالْحَقِّ أَتْقَنَ صُنْعَهَا

وَأَوْدَعَهَا الْأَسْرَارَ لِلَّهِ تَشْهَدُ

And for the certain, in the Earth are signs

that do not benefit those who reject.

And in the body, amazing designs

by which He is known and worshipped direct.

These many great signs confer and attest,

a glorious God, whose grace is untold!

And from His seedlings, fulfills their request.

No bliss will be found for those who withhold.

وَفِي الْأَرْضِ آيَاتٌ لِمَنْ كَانَ مُوقِنًا

وَمَا تَنْفَعُ الْآيَاتُ مَنْ كَانَ يَجْحَدُ

وَفِي النَّفْسِ آيَاتٌ وَفِيهَا عَجَائِبُ

بِهَا يُعْرَفُ اللَّهُ الْعَظِيمُ وَيُعْبَدُ

لَقَدْ قَامَتِ الْآيَاتُ تَشْهَدُ أَنَّهُ

إِلَهٌ عَظِيمٌ فَضْلُهُ لَيْسَ يَنْفَدُ

فَمَنْ كَانَ مِنْ غَرْسِ الْإِلَهِ أَجَابَهُ

وَلَيْسَ لِمَنْ وَلَّى وَأَدْبَرَ مُسْعِدُ

Keep your duty fulfilling His decree,

and from the forbidden you must steer clear,

avoid showing off, sincere you should be,

to the Prophet's way of worship adhere.

Trust The Merciful, a trust that is sure

to suffice your needs and guide you aright.

From sin and His rule, a must to endure.

And in submission you hope for delight.

عَلَيْكَ بِتَقْوَى اللهِ فِي فِعْلِ أَمْرِهِ

وَتَجْتَنِبُ الْمَنْهِيَّ عَنْهُ وَتَبْعُدُ

وَكُنْ مُخْلِصًا لِلّهِ وَاحْذَرْ مِنَ الرِّيَا

وَتَابِعْ رَسُولَ اللهِ إِنْ كُنْتَ تَعْبُدُ

تَوَكَّلْ عَلَى الرَّحْمنِ حَقًّا وَثِقْ بِهِ

لِيَكْفِيكَ مَا يُغْنِيكَ حَقًّا وَتَرْشُدُ

تَصَبَّرْ عَنِ الْعِصْيَانِ وَاصْبِرْ لِحُكْمِهِ

وَصَابِرْ عَلَى الطَّاعَاتِ عَلَّكَ تَسْعَدُ

Between fear and hope you are to proceed,

like wings of a bird in purpose and aim.

From every disease, your heart must be freed.

Always look to remove blemish and shame.

And adorn your heart by being sincere

to all mankind, a most lovely effect.

Those granted success, you make them your peer.

They lead you to good, and truly direct.

وَكُنْ سَائِرًا بَيْنَ الْمَخَافَةِ وَالرَّجَا

هُمَا كَجَنَاحَيْ طَائِرٍ حِينَ تَقْصِدُ

وَقَلْبَكَ طَهِّرْهُ وَمِنْ كُلِّ آفَةٍ

وَكُنْ أَبَدًا عَنْ عَيْبِهِ تَتَفَقَّدُ

وَجَمِّلْ بِنُصْحِ الْخَلْقِ قَلْبَكَ إِنَّهُ

لَأَعْلَى جَمَالٍ لِلْقُلُوبِ وَأَجْوَدُ

وَصَاحِبْ إِذَا صَاحَبْتَ كُلَّ مُوَفَّقٍ

يَقُودُكَ لِلْخَيْرَاتِ نُصْحًا وَيُرْشِدُ

And beware with whom, all your time, you spend

they cause you to lose, a loss that is true.

Pardon the manner of those you befriend

as The Most Gracious commands us to do.

Abandon this world, no place to abide.

A mere provision for those supplying.

Take those who preceded to be your guide

to the lasting home, ever undying.

وَإِيَّاكَ وَالْمَرْءَ الَّذِي إِنْ صَحِبْتَهُ

خَسِرْتَ خَسَارًا لَيْسَ فِيهِ تَرَدُّدُ

خُذِ الْعَفْوَ مِنْ أَخْلَاقِ مَنْ قَدْ صَحِبْتَهُ

كَمَا يَأْمُرُ الرَّحْمَنُ فِيهِ وَيُرْشِدُ

تَرَحَّلْ عَنِ الدُّنْيَا فَلَيْسَتْ إِقَامَةً

وَلَكِنَّهَا زَادٌ لِمَنْ يَتَزَوَّدُ

وَكُنْ سَالِكًا طُرْقَ الَّذِينَ تَقَدَّمُوا

إِلَى الْمَنْزِلِ الْبَاقِي الَّذِي لَيْسَ يَنْفَدُ

27

Praise and extol Him, regardless your state

Allah's remembrance, by time is unbound.

Mention the Lord of the throne who is great

Removes your sorrow if silent or sound.

For now and later, it earns much blessing,

repels the devil and keeps him at bay.

The Chosen told his comrades professing,

who praises the most is leading the way!

وَكُنْ ذَاكِرًا لِلَّهِ فِي كُلِّ حَالَةٍ

فَلَيْسَ لِذِكْرِ اللَّهِ وَقْتٌ مُقَيَّدُ

فَذِكْرُ إِلَهِ الْعَرْشِ سِرًّا وَمُعْلَنًا

يُزِيلُ الشَّقَا وَالْهَمَّ عَنْكَ وَيَطْرُدُ

وَيَجْلِبُ لِلْخَيْرَاتِ دُنْيَا وَآجِلًا

وَإِنْ يَأْتِكَ الْوَسْوَاسُ يَوْمًا يُشَرِّدُ

فَقَدْ أَخْبَرَ الْمُخْتَارُ يَوْمًا لِصَحْبِهِ

بِأَنَّ كَثِيرَ الذِّكْرِ فِي السَّبْقِ مُفْرِدُ

Seek support from your God, he did suggest

Mu'ādh, for praise, thanks, and worship so fine.

And one seeking advice at his request,

struggling with the law, to toe the line.

To keep your tongue moist mentioning His name.

Will help in all things, giving you pleasure.

With his mention, you plant seedlings to claim,

in Eden with homes prepared as treasure.

وَوَصَّى مُعَاذًا يَسْتَعِينُ إِلَهَهُ

عَلَى ذِكْرِهِ وَالشُّكْرِ بِالْحُسْنِ يَعْبُدُ

وَأَوْصَى لِشَخْصٍ قَدْ أَتَى لِنَصِيحَةٍ

وَقَدْ كَانَ فِي حَمْلِ الشَّرَائِعِ يَجْهَدُ

بِأَنْ لَا يَزَلْ رَطْبًا لِسَانُكَ هَذِهِ

تَعِينُ عَلَى كُلِّ الْأُمُورِ وَتُسْعِدُ

وَأَخْبَرَ أَنَّ الذِّكْرَ غَرْسٌ لِأَهْلِهِ

بِجَنَّاتِ عَدْنٍ وَالْمَسَاكِنُ تُمَهَّدُ

And said that Allāh will mention in phrase,

His servant, with him, directing his way.

And in Paradise will remain that praise.

Though his burden ends when ordered to stay.

And if naught else but the way to God's love,

guidance is found in the praise of His name.

Bans backbiting, slander, and all words of

Evil, which spoil faith and are of great blame.

وَأَخْبَرَ أَنَّ اللَّهَ يَذْكُرُ عَبْدَهُ

وَمَعْهُ عَلَى كُلِّ الْأُمُورِ يُسَدِّدُ

وَأَخْبَرَ أَنَّ الذِّكْرَ يَبْقَى بِجَنَّةٍ

وَيَنْقَطِعُ التَّكْلِيفُ حِينَ يُخَلَّدُوا

وَلَوْ لَمْ يَكُنْ فِي ذِكْرِهِ غَيْرَ أَنَّهُ

طَرِيقٌ إِلَى حُبِّ الْإِلَهِ وَمُرْشِدُ

وَيَنْهَى الْفَتَى عَنْ غِيبَةٍ وَنَمِيمَةٍ

وَعَنْ كُلِّ قَوْلٍ لِلدِّيَانَةِ مُفْسِدُ

A greater desire we would possess,

to increase His praise; the best singled out.

Due to our blindness it has become less,

and worship of Him; diminished to drought.

For gain and success, always ask your Lord.

Seeking his Master, not wronged is the slave.

For peace and mercy, ask God to reward

the best of creatures, great guidance he gave.

لَكَانَ لَنَا حَظٌّ عَظِيمٌ وَرَغْبَةٌ

بِكَثْرَةِ ذِكْرِ اللهِ نِعْمَ الْمُوَحَّدُ

وَلَكِنَّنَا مِنْ جَهْلِنَا قَلَّ ذِكْرُنَا

كَمَا قَلَّ مِنَّا لِلْإِلَهِ التَّعَبُّدُ

وَسَلْ رَبَّكَ التَّوْفِيقَ وَالْفَوْزَ دَائِمًا

فَمَا خَابَ عَبْدٌ لِلْمُهَيْمِنِ يَقْصِدُ

وَصَلِّ إِلَهِي مَعْ سَلَامٍ وَرَحْمَةٍ

عَلَى خَيْرِ مَنْ قَدْ كَانَ لِلْخَلْقِ يُرْشِدُ

His kin and comrades and those who pursue

Lasting prayers and peace; eternal, anew.

All praise is for Allāh.

وَآلٍ وَأَصْحَابٍ وَمَنْ كَانَ تَابِعًا

صَلَاةً وَتَسْلِيمًا يَدُومُ وَيَخْلُدُ

تَمَّ وَالْحَمْدُ لِلَّهِ.

Bibliography

al-Badr, A. R.-M. (n.d.). *Sharh Manhaj al-Haqq*.

al-Saʿdī, ʿ. a.-R. (2000). *Manhaj al-Salikin wa Tawdih al-Fiqh fi al-Din*. Riyad: Dar al-Watan.

al-Suhaymi, S. (2013). Sharh Manhaj al-Haqq. Madinah, KSA.

About the Translator

Abu Ibrāhīm John Starling is a graduate of the Islamic University of Madinah, KSA. He is an avid student of the Islamic sciences and has sought knowledge both formally and traditionally since 2001. He also possesses a degree in Business Management from NC State University, USA.

Made in the USA
Middletown, DE
15 November 2020